COOKING
LUNCH & DINNER

Asha Rani Vohra

V&S PUBLISHERS

Published by:

V&S PUBLISHERS

F-2/16, Ansari road, Daryaganj, New Delhi-110002
☎ 23240026, 23240027 • *Fax:* 011-23240028
Email: info@vspublishers.com • *Website:* www.vspublishers.com

Regional Office : Hyderabad

5-1-707/1, Brij Bhawan (Beside Central Bank of India Lane)
Bank Street, Koti, Hyderabad - 500 095
☎ 040-24737290
E-mail: vspublishershyd@gmail.com

Branch Office : Mumbai

Jaywant Industrial Estate, 1st Floor–108, Tardeo Road
Opposite Sobo Central Mall, Mumbai – 400 034
☎ 022-23510736
E-mail: vspublishersmum@gmail.com

Follow us on:

CONTENTS

Publisher's Note

The Indian housewife today is no longer the same as she was in the bygone days, who spent half of her life working in the kitchen with a back bent. Except for cooking, women of olden age living in the interior of their houses had no direct connection with their guests and almost no ambition in life.

Now she is a conscious housewife or a working woman, useful for the society. Progress in science and technology has made her world trouble-free. She herself wants to move with the times. She wishes to do her work better with the help of scientific equipments, technological ways and means, and gives her work an artistic touch, thus saving her labour and time which can be utilised further for other useful purposes. Such a training includes essential knowledge about food, efficient running of the kitchen and looking after it properly, cleanliness while cooking and serving food artistically, welcoming of guests and all modern etiquettes pertaining to it.

There are other books on culinary art and recipes available in the market. But this book is different from them.

An attempt has been made to cater to the metropolitan as well as the small town housewives. Problems arrive when parties and meals have to be organised. How to present the dishes artistically and tastefully before the guests is an important factor which should be considered. Guests should feel happy and the pleasure of eating enhances automatically.

The book *Cooking Lunch & Dinner* contains *recipes* with their ingredients and methods of preparation, special tip-offs and all the exclusive characteristics as mentioned above.

MOUTH-WATERING RECIPES

Tomato Soup

Tomato soup is not only tasty but very nutritious as well.

Tomato Soup

Ingredients

250 gms tomatoes
2 cups of water
salt (to taste)
2 tsps of sugar
2 black cardamoms
¼ tsp black pepper
2 tsps of butter

Method

Chop the tomatoes into pieces. Cook together two cups of water, salt, two spoons of sugar, one big chopped onion, two black cardamoms and black pepper, till the tomatoes and onions become tender. Take off from the fire. Wash and strain through a stainless steel sieve or clean thin cloth. Heat two spoons of butter in a vessel. Fry a spoon of flour in this on low heat. Then add the strained juice and cook for five minutes. Your soup is ready. It should be served in cups, absolutely hot. Small pieces of fried bread can be added to it just before serving. These should not be added earlier.

Tip off

You may add some basil leaves as garnishing to impart a special flavour to the soup.

Mixed Vegetable Soup

You can put any number of vegetables in this soup.

Mixed Vegetable Soup

Ingredients

2 tomatoes
2 carrots
2 spring onions
1 small bunch of spinach
2 to 3 leaves of cabbage
1 small radish with leaves or
a few pieces of radish along
with the edges of its leaves
½ cup of shelled peas
½ beetroot
1 or 2 green chillies
coriander leaves
3-4 leaves of mint

Method

Wash all the vegetables in water. Then cut them into small pieces. Cook in a cooker with water, salt, black pepper, cardamom, etc. till the vegetables are tender. Cooking in steam will preserve their vitamins. Take the cooker off the fire ten minutes after the pressure reaches the optimum level. Let it cool. Mash the vegetables and strain the soup. Now heat three or four spoons of butter in a vessel and fry one and half spoons of flour in it, on low fire. Put the strained soup and add two spoons of sugar. Cover the vessel and cook for ten minutes. Serve in cups, absolutely hot. You can add a pinch of salt or pepper according to your taste.

Tip off
A dash of lemon makes the soup
more tantalizing.

Japanese Mizutaki Soup ━━━━

The Japanese food is simple and nutritious.

Mizutaki Soup

Ingredients

8-10 pieces of chicken
(boneless preferred)
1 cup of sliced vegetables like
cabbage, carrots, French beans,
mushroom, etc.
1 tsp soya sauce
1 cup rice noodles
salt and pepper (to taste)

Method

Take a look at the picture. A special utensil with a chimney is used to prepare the Japanese Mizutaki Soup. The lower portion contains coal fire and the top is filled with water. Cook small pieces of chicken with salt in boiling water for ten minutes. The pieces should be partially tender. Put the cabbage, carrot, French beans and mushroom. More vegetables cut in pieces can also be used. The coal fire should be moderate by now, to be placed on the table. Finally add a little soya sauce and rice noodles in the soup and while it is being cooked on a low fire in the utensil with a chimney, take it to the dining table.

Tip off

Mizutaki Soup is cooked in a utensil with a chimney on the dining table.

Mutton Soup

Mutton soup is very healthy and tasty too if you are a non-vegetarian.

Mutton Soup

Ingredients

250 gms meat or mutton
2 onions
1 or 2 carrots
½ tsp sugar
1 egg
½ spoon fennel
4 cloves
2 large cardamoms
salt and pepper (to taste)
butter (to taste)

Method

Wash and clean the meat pieces well and put them in a vessel. Cook with carrots, pieces of onion, cardamoms, cloves, fennel and salt on a slow fire, with a lid, for two hours. Take down from the fire, wash and strain. The soup should look absolutely clear. Beat the white of an egg into a froth. Heat it up a little (do not boil). Strain with a cloth and mix the soup. Heat two tablespoons of butter in a vessel. Fry half a spoon of sugar till red. A few shelled peas can also be fried along with the sugar. Pour the soup and cook again on low fire for five minutes. Fried sugar will give it a red colour. While serving in cups or bowls, fried pieces of bread can also be added.

Tip off

This soup contains the nutritive value of meat and vegetables, both.

Greek Cheese Rolls

To make this dish vegetarian, do not add meat or chicken in the filling. If you are non-vegetarian, add minced/boiled meat in the filling

Greek Cheese Rolls

Ingredients

1 cup flour
3 tbsps grated cottage cheese (paneer)
¼ tsp salt
1 tbsp ghee
150 gms boiled potato
2 medium onions
½ cup boiled minced meat or
½ cup grated cottage cheese (paneer)
½ tbsp of booster sauce
coriander leaves
salt (to taste)
chopped green chillies (to taste)

Method

Mix flour, salt and sift. Add one spoon of ghee or butter to the grated cottage cheese (paneer). Knead sprinkling ice cold water. Store in the refrigerator for an hour. Take out and knead again. Make 15 to 16 balls. For the filling, peel potatoes and mash. Add the grated cottage cheese, chopped green coriander and salt.

Fry the chopped onions in ghee in a fry pan. When red, add the chopped green chillies and the booster sauce. Add the boiled minced meat or paneer and fry. Sprinkle salt and remove from the fire.

Heat ghee in a vessel. Roll a *puri* out of the prepared dough. Spread potato mixture on each *puri* with a spoon. Spread fried or minced meat or *paneer* on the top and roll each *puri* in a round shape. Stick the sides with flour batter. Toothpicks can also be used to stick them. Fry each roll separately in a vessel.

Decorate on a plate and serve with tomato sauce, white sauce.

Tip off

It is a delicious dish for tea and cocktails. It can be used as a tantalizing starter too!

String Hoppers

The shape of string hoppers is similar to the popular momos of today but their taste is different.

String Hoppers

Ingredients

1 cup rice flour
¼ tsp mustard seed
250 gms minced meat orf cottage cheese or boiled vegetables
¼ tsp poppy seed
100 gms potato
¼ tsp cumin seed
100 gms onion
4 flakes garlic
3 green chillies
¼ tsp ground aniseed
1 lime
2 tbsp of tomato sauce
1 tsp of *garam masala*
salt and ghee (to taste)

Method

Add one cup of rice flour to about one-fourth cup of boiling water, gradually. Put a pinch of salt, stir rapidly and bring down from the fire. When cool knead and wrap in a wet cloth. Keep aside. After some time, knead again and make small balls one by one. Put them in a small cake mould (a big vessel will also do) and press with a wet palm in the shape of small bowls (like cake moulds.) Place them on a sieve. Now place them on a big vessel of boiling water and cook in steam.

Fry half of the chopped onion or one whole onion in a vessel in ghee. Put chopped green chillies, ground poppy seeds, aniseeds, mustard and cumin seeds. Fry the ground garlic a little. Then put the minced meat. Add salt, water and cook. Fry on low fire. When the minced meat is tender and water evaporates, squeeze juice of half a lime. Add the *garam masala* powder and bring it down from the fire. Instead of minced/boiled meat, you can use minced cottage cheese also.

Cut the rest of the onions in rings and fry them in ghee or butter. Peel the potatoes and mash them. Fry them also in ghee and put a pinch of salt.

Arrange the rice flour moulds and fill them with fried minced meat or cottage cheese. Place one thick fried onion ring on each. Now fill it with fried potato filling. Decorate with lines of tomato sauce. Place all the saucers in a greased baking dish and bake in an oven or microwave .

Tip off

Rice flour can either be bought from a departmental store or by grinding some dry rice grams at home.

Cheese Stars ———

These baked cheese stars are tasty, healthy and low in calories.

Cheese Stars

Ingredients

4 spoons corn flour
4 tbsps of butter or of salad oil
4 tbsps of wheat flour
6 tbsps of grated cottage
cheese or 1 egg
salt, red chilli powder
and black pepper (to taste)

Method

Sift the wheat flour and corn flour together.

Knead with salad oil or butter. Mix the cottage cheese and spices. Break open the egg, add the yellow yolk and knead. If the dough seems hard, add one and half spoons of milk to soften it. Roll like a *chapatti*. Cut squares with a knife, or cut like round biscuits with a round lid. You may even cut it in star shape using a stencil.

Grease the baking tray with butter or ghee as per your convenience. Put the cut pieces on it and bake in low heat. Serve hot with tea or coffee.

Tip off

You may garnish each cheese star with parsley, coriander and onion rings.

Paneer Tikka

Paneer tikka is relished hot and steaming.

Paneer Tikka

Ingredients

500 gms *paneer*
(cottage cheese)
1 onion
1 capsicum
1 tomato
few mushrooms (optional)
finely chopped coriander leaves

To Marinate:
½ cup curd (plain yogurt)
1 tsp garlic paste
1 tsp ginger paste
2 tsp tandoori powder
1 tsp cumin powder
2 tsp chaat powder
salt (to taste)
red chilli powder

Method

Cut *paneer* into long half inch thick cubes. Cut all the vegetables mentioned in the ingredients into cubes. Mix all the ingredients for marinating and keep the mixture aside. Brush the marinated mixture to the *paneer* and refrigerate it for three hours. Place the *paneer* and vegetable pieces on the barbeque stick and place them in the tandoor. Keep rotating the stick so that they are well done from all sides. In a plate, arrange the vegetables and *paneer*, when done. Garnish with coriander leaves and lemon slice.

Tip off

Serve the tandoori *paneer* tikka hot
with green chutney made up of mint
and coriander leaves.

Fish Chops

Fish chops are relished even by those who do not like the smell of fish.

Fish Chops

Ingredients

250 gms fish
175 gms potato
2 medium onions
1 egg or 2 eggs
½ bowl bread crumbs
1 tbsp sugar
ginger
garlic
salt, green chillies, *garam masala*, ghee or oil (to taste)

Method

Boil the potatoes, peel and mash them carefully. Cut the fish and boil it. Put one spoon of salt in the boiling water. When tender take out the bones and mash the fish. Grind an onion, ginger and garlic. Cut one onion in long, thin slices. Fry the sliced onion well in ghee, add the ground spices and cook on slow fire till the ghee/oil separates. Add the fish, fry for about five minutes and remove from fire. Mix together salt, chillies chopped coriander, boiled potatoes and shape into cubes. Put the fish in the middle and shape into longish chops. Beat an egg in a flat deep plate. Dip the fish potato chops in it, roll in bread crumbs and fry them in ghee or oil. Your fish chops are ready to eat.

Tip off

You can use mustard oil to fry the fish chops in place of refined, oil, butter or ghee.

Fried Pomfret Fish

Pomfret fish does not have too many bones, so it is easy and tasty to eat.

Fried Pomfret Fish

Ingredients

1 medium size pomfret fish
1 cup curd
1 lime
1 onion
ginger
salt, chillies, turmeric, *garam masala*, ghee or oil (to taste)

Method

Clean the fish and keep it whole. Put deep lines with a knife here and there. Grind onion and ginger. Add all the spices to curd and stuff in the fish. Then keep aside for an hour. Afterwards, deep fry in ghee or refined oil, turning sides, first on high flame and then on slow fire, till done and crisp. You may squeeze lime juice on top. After adding the lime juice, sprinkle *garam masala* and chopped coriander leaves. You can also use mustard oil to fry the pomfret fish.

Tip off

Put the whole fried pomfret on a big plate. Put the fish chops on another fish shaped flat plate and put a fish shaped flower vase along with it. These two delicacies made with fish will be an attraction for your guests and make the table look livelier.

Tandoori Chicken

Tandoori chicken should be properly roasted and made crisp before serving.

Ingredients

1 medium size chicken
2 tsp lime juice
ghee
onion
garlic
ginger
salt
green chillies
garam masala (to taste)

Tandoori Chicken

Method

Grind together ginger, garlic and onion. Add curd to make a batter. Coat the chicken well from all sides with this batter. Keep aside and let it dry for five minutes. Now wet grind cumin seeds, chillies, salt, adding the lime juice. Fill the chicken from every side with this paste. Keep aside for one hour.

Pass the Kabab sticks through the chicken. Put ghee, butter or oil on top and roast in special mud oven, known as *tandoor*. Sprinkle chopped coriander and *garam masala* after the chicken is done.

Tip off

Tandoori chicken tastes better if served with lime, onion and salads.

Shaami Kabab

Shaami kababs may be roasted or shallow fried, depending upon your taste.

Shaami Kabab

Ingredients

1 cup *gram dal*
250 gms minced meat or chicken
1 or 2 big onion
3 green chillies
3 garlic flakes
½ inch piece ginger
¼ tsp ground rind of lime
¼ tsp cumin seeds
4 cloves
¼ tsp ground cinnamon
¼ tsp ground pepper
coriander leaves
salt and ghee or
refined oil (to taste)

Method

Soak the gram dal overnight. Grind coarsely in the morning. Chop the onions, garlic, ginger, coriander leaves, green chillies finely. Except a round ring of lime, add the rest of the spices to minced the meat and mix well. Add the *dal* paste also.

Make round balls of the size of big lime. Place the round rind of lime in the middle and roll the ball into a longish shape. Fry them in ghee or refined oil till red. Serve with onions, cucumbers, tomatoes or *chutney*.

Tip off

Shaami kababs can be made in any shape you like. Always use a non-stick frying pan to make any fried food item.

Seekh Kabab

You can make seekh kabab without chicken using only mutton.

Ingredients

250 gm chicken and mutton
1 lemon
1 tsp poppy seeds
2 black cardamoms
3 cloves
½ tsp cinnamon powder
½ tsp coriander powder
½ tsp red chilli powder
¼ ground pepper
2 or 3 medium sized onions
garlic, green chillies, coriander
leaves, salt and ghee
or oil (to taste)

Seekh Kabab

Method

Grind the onions and garlic to a paste. Fry in ghee or refined oil. Add the red chilli powder, coriander, cardamom, cloves, pepper seeds and the cinnamon powder. Add the minced chicken or mutton, chopped coriander leaves, green chillies, black pepper, salt and lime juice. Turn a bit and remove from the fire. Grease the iron rods with ghee and put this mixture on it, in the shape of kababs. Then roast on slow coal fire. Keep on applying ghee or oil to it with a clean piece of cloth.

After the kabab is roasted red, take out of the rod and serve hot. They are delicious if served with salads, curd and mint *chutney*.

Tip off

You can eat the seekh kababs by rolling it in a thin *rumali roti*. This is basically an Afghani food.

Mince Cakes

Mince cakes are *salted cakes*, not sweet.

Mince Cakes

Ingredients

250 gms minced meat or cottage cheese
125 gms gram flour (besan)
1 big onion
2 green chillies
¼ tsp red chilli powder
¼ tsp *garam masala*
1 inch piece ginger
amchoor (dried mango powder)
coriander leaves
salt (to taste)
ghee or refined oil (for frying)

Method

Wash the mince and put in a cooker. Vegetarians can use cottage cheese (paneer). Add a pinch of salt and cook. Add the *gram dal* powder, chopped green chillies, coriander leaves, finely chopped onion, ginger. Add the red chilli powder, *garam masala* and *amchoor* and salt. Make small balls. Flatten them and fry them on a *tawa* or frying pan as in potato cakes. Cook it direct on slow fire for a long time till red. They can be fried in ghee in a vessel also. Serve with salads and *chutney*.

Decoration

Take a round but small sized cucumber and cut it into two halves with a knife in zig-zag shape. Separate the two parts and empty them from the middle. Now you have two bowls made of zig-zag cucumber. Fill one with mint *chutney* and the other with tomato sauce and place them on the plate of mince cakes. You can use a longish tray lined up on four sides with mince cakes. The centre can have two cucumber bowls with *chutney* and a boy doll can be made of boiled potatoes. The doll's cap with a feather on top is made out of a beetroot ring. Eyes and nose can be made by inserting cloves and the mouth can have bits of sliced tomato.

Tip off

Such bowls of cucumber can be decorated on a plate of kababs also.

Patato-Mince Patties

To make these patties more attractive, you may decorate them with onions cut in the shape of flowers.

Potato-Mince Patties

Ingredients

250 gms minced meat or cottage (paneer)
250 gms potatoes
1 egg
½ cup bread crumbs
2 medium sized onions
salt, red chilli powder, chopped green chillies,
coriander leaves, *garam masala*, lemon (to taste)
ghee or refined oil (for frying)

Method

Boil potatoes, peel and mash. Heat the ghee or refined oil in a vessel or a frying pan. Add finely chopped onions and fry. Put the minced meat or *paneer* and fry. Add a little water and salt. Cook till the mince is tender. Add enough water to be absorbed. Put the mince on low fire, add *garam masala*, chopped green chillies and the coriander leaves. Then fry till reddish brown. Add the juice of half a lemon and remove from fire.

Add the juice of the remaining half a lemon to the mashed potatoes. Add salt, red chilli powder and the coriander leaves.

Make almond sized balls from this mixture. Make a hollow in the middle with your hand. Stuff the fried mince in it and make round patties. Beat an egg. Dip each patty separately in the whipped egg, roll in bread crumbs and fry in ghee or refined oil. Serve the hot patties with mint *chutney* or tomato sauce.

Tip off

To avoid too much fat in frying, you may roast or bake the patties in an oven. You can avoid using red chilli powder if you prefer it less spicy.

Wonder Mutton Chops ———

This plate of chops may be decorated with a waiter-doll made of three boiled potatoes placed on top of each other. Cucumbers, tomatoes and cloves may be used to decorate the dolls' face.

Wonder Mutton Chops

Ingredients

6 longish big mutton chops (boneless mutton pieces)
2 or 3 onions
250 gms potatoes
1 egg
2 big tomatoes
2 cloves
2 large cardamoms
1 inch piece of ginger
6 flakes of garlic
½ cup vinegar
½ cup bread crumbs
black pepper, ghee or refined oil, salt and red chilli powder (to taste)

Method

Wash and clean the mutton chops or boneless mutton pieces. Chop the onions finely. Grind garlic and ginger to a paste. Marinate the chops in grounded spices of ginger, garlic, onions and *garam masala*. Soak in vinegar for two hours. Take out and boil them in a cooker with enough water, till soft and the water evaporates or a little bit is left. Boil the potatoes, peel and mash. Add the tomato pulp, salt, red chilli powder, chopped coriander, finely cut onions and *garam masala* to the mashed potatoes.

Now fill the empty part of a mutton chop with this mixture and press with your hand. The thin bones of the chops should be sticking out on one side. Fill the rest of the mashed potatoes similarly and shape the chops. Beat an egg with a pinch of salt and beat hard into a froth. Dip the chops in the egg batter, roll them in bread crumbs and fry in a vessel or frying pan in hot ghee or oil, turning sides.

Tip off

Place a waiter made from boiled potato salads and toothpicks in the middle of the chops along with lots of salads and *chutney* to make the dish look really attractive!

Tri-Colour

Tri-colour may be decorated with tiny flowers made of carrots.

Tri-colour

Ingredients

1 cup washed *moong dal* (split green gram)
1 cup shelled green peas
cottage cheese or *paneer* (in proportion)
green chillies, salt,
red chilli powder (optional),
turmeric (to taste)
1 carrot
ghee or oil (as required)

Method

Cook the *dal* in enough water to evaporate when the *dal* is tender. Add salt, turmeric and the red chilli powder while cooking. Take out from the vessel. Add ghee, butter or oil and fry lightly. Add a little turmeric to the ghee while frying, for a nice yellow colour.

Pound the shelled peas and the green chillies together. Heat a little ghee in a vessel or frying pan and add the pounded peas. Sprinkle water and cook with salt. When tender, fry on low fire till a little dry. Add salt and a few drops of lemon juice to the cottage cheese or *paneer*. Knead well. Fry in ghee separately. Now you have ingredients of three different colours – *yellow dal*, *green peas* and the *white cottage cheese* (paneer).

Grease a shallow box or lunch box with ghee or butter. Now put a layer of *cottage cheese* first, then arrange a layer of *peas* on it and then a layer of *dal* on top. Even out the top with hands. Leave it for a while till it sets. Now upturn the box on a plate. Tri-colour Dish is ready with yellow at the bottom, green in the centre and white on top. You may place the three layers in a different order also.

Tip off

This tri-colour vegetarian dish is rich in proteins, hence full of nutrition. Its attractive look will enhance the beauty of your dining table. Just cut it into pieces with a knife and serve.

Cauliflower Musallam

Cauliflower is an all season vegetable. Cook it in a different way, especially for your guests. It will be tasty and also look good on the table.

Cauliflower Musallam

Ingredients

A middle sized cauliflower
4 onions
2 tomatoes
4 green chillies
coriander leaves
spices
ginger
lettuce leaves for decoration
ghee or oil (for frying)

Method

Remove the stem and leaves from the cauliflower. Wash and dry the whole cauliflower and cook it in ghee or oil on low flame. Sprinkle ghee with a spatula on the upper part. Take out, draining all the ghee, when it becomes light red and tender.

Take out the extra ghee in a bowl and fry the onion, garlic, ginger and ground spices in it. When red, add pieces of peeled tomato and cook on low fire for a little while. Add the turmeric and red chillie powder first and salt and *garam masala* after the spices are fully fried. Now take off this mixture of spices from the fire and stuff it well in the cauliflower cooking it again for five minutes on low fire, covered with a lid.

Now spread the lettuce leaves on the plate (tender leaves of cauliflower can also be used). Place the spicy cauliflower in the centre and decorate with coriander leaves and green chillies.

Tip off

As the upper part is softer, it will cook well if the stem side of the cauliflower is placed downwards.

Stuffed Tomatoes ————————

Tomatoes are used to give flavour to the vegetables. When you cook, make them stuffed, they will make a delicious dish for the guests and also look good on the table.

Stuffed Tomatoes

Ingredients

8 middle sized firm red tomatoes
250 gms potatoes
spices
green chillies
coriander leaves
ghee or oil (as necessary)
1 tsp flour

Method

Wash the tomatoes and wipe them dry. Cut small rings from the top of each tomato. Take out the pulp from inside by scraping carefully. Keep the rings aside.

Boil, peel and mash the potatoes. Mix the tomato pulp with it.

Add chopped green chillies, red chilli powder (optional), *garam masala*, turmeric powder and coriander leaves. Fill the hollow in the tomatoes with this mixture and cover them with rings. Make a thick batter of flour. Add a pinch of salt and close the opening along the cover.

Put enough ghee or oil in a vessel to soak the tomatoes. Fry on a high flame fast and take out. Take care that the tomatoes remain whole.

Now place the tomatoes on a plate and sprinkle the chopped coriander leaves on top of the stuffing. This dish will be pleasing to the eyes and delicious to eat.

Tip off

While frying, the tomatoes need not be cooked till tender, so there is no need to lower the flame. If the tomatoes are overcooked, they can break and the potato filling can spill out.

Parval Boats

Parval or snake gourd is a nutritious vegetable. If cooked and decorated properly, it will be liked by those also who did not care much for this vegetable earlier, and they will benefit from its goodness.

Ingredients

8 *parvals* or snake gourds
2 tomatoes
2 onions
spices
a piece of radish
ghee or oil

Parval Boats

Method

Wash the *parvals* or the snake gourds and dry. Cut into two pieces from the middle. Heat the ghee or oil and fry the *parvals*, first on a high flame and then on low fire. Remove.

Grind the onions and other spices. Fry in ghee or oil. Add the turmeric and red chilli powder. Then add the tomato pulp and fry. Now add enough water to make a thick gravy. Cook the gravy with salt and *garam masala* on low heat for about five minutes.

Remove the gravy on a long plate and place the *parval* pieces on it like a row of boats. Cut triangular thin pieces from the radish and place them on these boats to look like sails.

Tip off

Parvals or Snake Gourds sailing on the gravy will look like boats sailing in a river.

Capsicums Cooked in Curd

Try this new recipe with small sized capsicums. You will surely like it.

Capsicums in Curd

Ingredients

8 small capsicums
1 cup of curd
spices
ghee
small amount of cottage cheese
(paneer)

Method

Wash the capsicums and cut them in halves. Now fry them in heated ghee or refined oil on a high flame. Then remove from the fire. Tie the curd in a cloth and hang. When drained, take out and mix turmeric, salt and a pinch of red chilli powder. Now stuff this mixture well in the capsicums. Then cook with a lid on low fire. Remove and decorate on a plate. Garnish with grated cottage cheese (paneer) and chopped coriander leaves.

Tip off

You may add chopped mushrooms, carrots, cabbage, etc. in the curd for filling in the capsicums.

Vegetable Mince

This preparation is tasty as well as very healthy for the human body. You can use as many vegetables as you like to make it more nutritious.

Vegetable Mince

Ingredients

A medium cauliflower
4 onions
1 inch piece of ginger
8 to 10 flakes of garlic
2 tomatoes
ground spices or use powdered spices
1 or 2 radish cut in pieces
pieces of carrots
ghee or refined oil

Method

Wash the whole cauliflower and dry. Grate. Grind the onion, garlic and ginger and make a paste of it. Fry the spices in good quantity of ghee or refined oil. Add the tomato pulp, chillie powder and the onions till it becomes red. Now add the grated cauliflower and put salt on top. Cook the cauliflower on low heat, covered with a lid. See that it does not become too tender. Fry like mince and remove from the fire.

Put it on a plate. Sprinkle *garam masala* and chopped coriander leaves to garnish your preparation. Then decorate with flowers cut out of radish and carrots.

Tip off

You can make similar vegetable mince with soyabean also. Soyabean granules like mince are available in the market. Soak them in water for 15 to 20 minutes before cooking.

Cottage Cheese in Spinach

This is one of the most popular dishes of North India. It is a special vegetarian dish relished in occasions and functions, even.

Cottage Cheese in Spinach or Palak Paneer

Ingredients

500 gms spinach or *palak*
200-250 gms cottage cheese (paneer)
1 or 2 tomatoes
4 flakes of garlic
a small piece of ginger
salt
green chillies
ghee or oil (as per taste)

Method

Clean and wash the spinach (palak). Chop it. Grind the onion, garlic and ginger in a fine paste. Peel the tomatoes and cut it into pieces. Cut the cottage cheese (paneer) into small triangular, square or rectangular pieces and fry them slightly in ghee or oil. Keep aside.

Put the spinach (palak) with a little water and salt in a pressure cooker and cook for about five minutes after it reaches the required pressure. The remaining water should not be more than a bowl. Strain this water and keep aside. Grind the spinach finely. Now fry the onions in ghee till red. Then add the ginger, garlic, tomato pieces, red chilli powder and fry for some more time. Now add the ground spinach and the fried pieces of cottage cheese. Stir. Add the strained spinach water to make the consistency thinner. Keep on low fire for about five minutes and remove. Decorate with a few pieces of cottage cheese.

Tip off

Cottage cheese in spinach is a highly appreciated dish because of its palatability and nutritional values. It is commonly called *palak paneer.*

Dried Thickened Milk and Cashew Nuts

This is an expensive, nutritious and rich preparation, often made for guests on special occasions. Cook it with aniseeds and cardamoms to give it a distinctive taste and also to make it easily digestible.

Dried thickened milk and cashew nuts

Ingredients

200 gms dried thickened milk
100 gms cashew nuts
50 gms raisins
2 onions
5 flakes of garlic
1 inch piece of ginger
1 large tomato or 2 medium sized tomatoes
1 tsp aniseeds
3 black cardamoms
turmeric
salt
red chilli powder
coriander leaves
garam masala (as per taste)

Method

Boil the cashews once after soaking in water. Strain and separate the cashews. Clean the raisins. Pound the aniseeds and the cardamom seeds. Cut the onion rings finely. Grind the ginger and the garlic. Chop the coriander leaves.

Heat ghee or oil in a vessel and fry the onion rings. Add the ginger-garlic paste, when light red. Fry a little and then add turmeric, red chilli powder, tomato pulp and boiled water of cashew nuts. Cook on a high flame for about five minutes. Lower the heat and cook the spices till the ghee separates. Now add dried thickened milk and fry. Add the cashews, raisins, aniseeds, cardamoms, salt and cook on low fire covered with a lid. Sprinkle chopped coriander leaves and *garam masala* after five minutes and remove from the fire. Decorate the plate with few more cashew nuts.

Tip off

This dish cannot be consumed in large amounts, so cook it in moderate quantities and serve accordingly.

Sai Bhaji ────────

This popular dish is a mixture of many vegetables, rich in mineral salts, vitamins and proteins. It contains the highly proteinacous *gram dal*.

Sai Bhaji

Ingredients

100 gms *gram dal*
200 gms spinach (palak)
coriander leaves
a bunch of sour leafy vegetables
1 brinjal
1 pumpkin
cauliflower
a middle-sized potato
1 or 2 carrots
1 tomato
1 or 2 onions
5 to 6 flakes of garlic
1 piece of ginger
green chillies
coriander powder
salt (as per taste)
ghee / oil as cooking medium

Method

Pressure cook the *gram dal* in one cup of water. Keep on fire for about two minutes after the pressure reaches the optimum level. Wash and cut all the vegetables. Open the cooker after it cools. Add all the vegetables and spices to the partially cooked *dal*. Close the cooker and cook on pressure for around five minutes. Now mash the vegetables and *dal* together. Cook on a low fire for about three minutes, closed with a lid. Then take out and decorate with radish leaves and grated cheese. Serve with rice.

Tip off

In case the sour leafy vegetable mentioned in the ingredients is not available, soak tamarind in water and use the water to give a sour taste.

Hariyali Butter Paneer

This dish has the softness of cottage cheese (paneer) and the flavour of capsicum.

Hariyali Butter Paneer

Ingredients

250 grams cottage cheese
(paneer)
1 tbsp lemon juice
1 tsp green chilli paste
1 tsp ginger paste
salt (to taste)
6 medium tomatoes
1 tbsp oil
4 stalks garlic (chopped)
1 green capsicum (deseeded
and chopped)
4 stalks spring onions with
greens chopped
4 tbsps white butter
5 cloves
3 green cardamoms
1 small stick cinnamon
3 tbsps of *mawa* (khoya)
1 tsp *garam masala* powder
½ cup fresh cream
½ tsp *kasoori methi*

Method

Blend the tomatoes to a puree. Set aside in a bowl. Marinate the cottage cheese (paneer) pieces with lemon juice, green chilli paste and salt for 15 minutes. Heat oil or ghee in a pan, add garlic, green capsicum and spring onions and sauté. Cool and blend to a puree. Set aside in a bowl. Heat the white butter in a pan. Add the cloves, cardamoms, cinnamon and sauté. Add chopped garlic ginger paste and sauté. Add the *khoya* and tomato puree and sauté. Now add capsicum puree and mix. Mix the *garam masala* powder, honey, salt and stir. Add marinated *paneer* pieces and mix. Now add fresh cream and stir gently. Sprinkle the *kasuri methi* and remove from heat. Mix gently and serve hot.

Tip off

To give it a better green colour,
you may use two-three leaves of
spinach.

Kashmiri Dum Aloo

There are different ways of cooking potato but this is the most favoured dish.

Kashmiri Dum Aloo

Ingredients

900 gms potatoes
ghee or oil (for deep-frying)
1 or 2 medium sized onions (finely chopped)
8 garlic flakes
2 tbsps ginger
4 tbsps of tomato puree, 140 ml curd
2 dry red chillies
1 tsp turmeric powder
a pinch of ground mace and nutmeg
1 or 2 tsps *garam masala* powder
(4 cloves, 4 bay leaves, 6 black peppercorns, 4 cardamoms and 1 piece cinnamon stick)
1 tsp poppy seeds
1 tbsp coriander seeds
1 tsp cumin seeds and salt to taste

Method

Scrape the potatoes and prick all over with a fork after soaking in the water with little salt for 2 hours. Dry the potatoes on a cloth and heat the ghee or oil. Deep fry the potatoes until golden brown. Drain and set aside. Heat the measured ghee in a flameproof pan and fry the onions with all the spices until brown in colour. Grind the ingredients to a smooth paste and stir into the onions. Cook for 10 minutes. Stir in the tomato puree, curd and salt. Add the potatoes and hot water and stir over a low heat for 5 minutes.

Sprinkle the *dum aloo* with pepper and *garam masala* and cook for a few minutes, if you want it more spicy. Garnish your recipe with coriander leaves.

Tip off

Use small sized potatoes for better taste and look.

Kadhai Paneer

This dish is best served in a brass *kadhai* (wok).

Kadhai Paneer

Ingredients

250 gms cottage cheese
(paneer)
3 capsicum
4 onions
4 tomatoes
a piece of ginger
1 tsp red chilli powder
2 bay leaves
4 cloves
1 piece of cinnamon
4 tbsps clarified butter (ghee)
or any refined oil or butter

Method

Cut the cottage cheese (paneer) and capsicum in long pieces. Grind the onions, tomatoes, ginger, salt, red chilli powder into paste. Mince the cloves and the cinnamon. Heat the clarified butter in a pan. Add the bay leaves, cloves and the cinnamon. Then add the onions, tomatoes, ginger paste. Continue cooking it on medium flame till the ghee/oil/ butter begins to separate. Add the *paneer* and capsicum pieces. Cook on low flame.

When the capsicums are done, put off the flame. Take off from the fire and serve hot.

Tip off

Do not reheat this dish many times,
otherwise the cottage cheese (paneer)
will lose its flavour.

Malai Kofta

Malai koftas are not entirely made of *malai*, as the name suggests, but they are as soft as *malai*.

Malai Kofta

Ingredients

1 1/2 lb. potatoes
2 heaped tbsp each of crumbled
paneer, *khoya* and thick *malai*
4-5 cashewnuts (chopped)
1 tbsp raisins, 2-3 finely chopped
green chillies, 1/4 tsp sugar
1 tsp coriander powder
1 tsp cumin powder
1 tsp red-chilli powder
1/2 tsp cardamom powder
salt to taste, 3 tbsp cooking
oil/ghee and oil for frying the *koftas*

Method

Boil the potatoes till tender. Peel, mash and add salt to taste. Keep aside. Mix all the other ingredients for the *kofta* into a paste. Make rounds of the potato dough and place a little of the prepared mixture in the centre of each round. Seal the edges and shape into stuffed rounds. Deep fry each *kofta* till golden brown. Drain and keep aside. Blend together the onions, ginger, garlic and the poppy seeds and fry in 3 tbsps of oil till brown and the oil begins to seperate. Add the pureed tomatoes and the *masala* powder. Add the sugar and the ground peanuts. The gravy will begin to thicken. You can also add some *malai* to thicken it some more. Mix in some water if necessary. When the gravy comes to a boil, add the koftas. Serve the *Malai Kofta* with Buttered Naan.

Tip off

In this Malai Kofta recipe, the Koftas should be put in the gravy just before eating the dish or else, they will turn soggy.

Chicken Curry

This dish is made with chicken. You may substitute chicken with mutton pieces to make mutton curry.

Chicken Curry

Ingredients

1 chicken medium size
200 gms onion
150 gms tomato
100 gms curd
Ginger, garlic, salt, coriander, chilli powder, turmeric, *garam masala* (as per taste)

Method

Cut the chicken into pieces and wash or get it cut from the meat shop. Heat ghee or refined oil in a cooker and fry ground onions. Add ginger, garlic paste, tomato, curd and fry till the ghee or oil separates. Now add turmeric, chilli powder, coriander and pieces of chicken. Fry till reddish brown. Add salt, water and close the cooker lid. Cook for 7 to 8 minutes after the pressure reaches the optimum limit. Bring the cooker down from fire and let it cool. Then open and serve. Sprinkle the *garam masala* and chopped coriander leaves on top to garnish the dish.

Tip off

For special flavour, you may add readymade chicken masala, available in the market to the curry.

Rogan Josh

It is a rich and delicious non-vegetarian dish. This is very popular in Jammu and Kashmir.

Rogan Josh

Ingredients

500 gms meat or mutton
1 small nutmeg
100 gms onions
1 small stick cinnamon
125 gms tomatoes
6 cloves
100 gms curd
20 gms grated coconut
15 almond pieces
12 flakes of garlic
3 kashmiri red chillies
15 gms ginger
2 black cardamoms
1 tsp cumin seeds
10 pepper seeds
1 tsp coriander seeds
½ tsp poppy seeds
turmeric, salt, ghee or oil (as per taste)
cashew nuts and coriander leaves for decoration

Method

Roast lightly the poppy seeds, coriander, cumin seeds, cardamoms, almonds, cloves, cinnamon, nutmeg and coconut. Soak the Kashmiri red chillies in half a cup of water for half an hour. Grind the roasted spices with ginger, garlic and the Kashmiri red chillies. Chop the onions finely.

Put ghee or oil in a cooker and fry the onions. Add the coarsely ground cardamoms and fry for another minute. Add the turmeric and ground spices and fry again. Add the tomato pulp and curd. After the tomato becomes tender, fry the spices again. Clean the meat and add to the spices. Fry till light red. Now add one cup of water and salt and close the cooker. Cook for 10 minutes after the pressure reaches the required limit. Open the cooker after it cools down. Transfer on a plate and garnish with chopped coriander leaves, *garam masala* and cashew nuts.

Tip off

Rogan Josh has a thick consistency, so eat it with nan or roti to get the right taste.

Mince Ball Curry

Mince balls in gravy is a delicious non-vegetarian dish.

Mince Ball Curry

Ingredients

250 gms minced meat or chicken
2 medium sized potatoes
2 big tomatoes
¼ coconut
1 lime
3 medium sized onions
1 ½ inch piece of ginger
4 flakes of garlic
½ tsp of poppy seeds
4 cloves
1 piece of cinnamon
2 red dry chillies
green chillies, salt, ghee or refined oil, coriander leaves (as per taste)

Method

Boil the potatoes, peel and mash. Fry and grind the minced meat or chicken, coconut and poppy seeds together. Add the mashed potatoes, lime and make into balls. Put ghee or refined oil in a vessel and fry the balls.

Now put the ghee or oil in a cooker and fry the chopped onions. Add the ginger garlic paste and fry. Add the tomato and cook till soft. Fry and add one cup of water. When water gets heated up, put the meat balls in it. Close the cooker. Cook for two minutes on low fire after the pressure reaches the optimum level. Cool the cooker. Remove the lid of the cooker and sprinkle *garam masala*, chopped coriander leaves, etc. in the gravy. The Mince Ball Curry can be served with both rice or *chapattis*.

Tip off

In Mince Ball Curry, soaked and ground *chana dal* can also be used in place of potatoes.

Goan Liver Curry

This is a popular Goan dish which has a special flavour of coconut and vinegar together.

Goan Liver Curry

Ingredients

300 gms liver
½ fresh coconut
3 cardamoms
3 sweet neem leaves
or 1 twig of sweet neem
1 tbsp vinegar
½ tsp fenugreek powder
4 red chillies
2 onions
5 flakes of garlic
1 inch piece of ginger

Method

Grind the aniseeds. Grate the coconut. Cook the red chillies in a little water and grind. Chop the onions. Grind the ginger and garlic.

Put the liver in a cooker with salt and water. After the pressure reaches on a high fire, lower the heat and cook for eight minutes. Take out the steam and open the cooker fast. Heat the ghee in a vessel and fry the onions. Add sweet neem leaves and ginger garlic paste. Put the red chilli powder, turmeric, fenugreek powder and ground aniseeds. Take out the liver from water and fry. Add the 'stock' (liver water) when red. Add the vinegar and cook for five minutes on low fire. Now switch off the fire. Decorate with chopped coriander leaves and mixed spice (*garam masala*). Serve with salads.

Tip off

To make it more spicy and tasty, fry the pieces of liver before cooking.

Butter Chicken

To prepare this dish for vegetarian guests, add cottage cheese (paneer) instead pf chicken pieces.

Butter Chicken

Ingredients

150 ml natural yogurt
50 gms ground almonds
1½ tsp chillie powder
¼ tsp crushed bay leaves
¼ tsp ground cloves
¼ tsp ground cinnamon
1tsp *garam masala*
4 green cardamom pods
1tsp ginger paste, 1 tsp garlic paste
400gms tomatoes
salt (to taste)
1kg chicken (skinned, boned and cubed)
75gms butter
1 tbsp oil
2 medium sized onions (sliced)
2 tbsps of fresh coriander (chopped)
4 tbsps of fresh cream

Method

Place the yogurt, ground almonds, all the dry spices, ginger, garlic, tomatoes and salt in a mixing bowl and blend together thoroughly to make the yogurt mixture. Put the chicken pieces into a large mixing bowl and pour the yogurt mixture over them. Set aside. Melt together the butter and oil in a *karahi*, or wok or a frying pan.

Add the onions and fry for about three minutes. Add the chicken mixture and stir-fry for about 7 to 10 minutes. Cook till the chicken is done. Stir in about half of the coriander and mix well. Pour over the cream and stir in well. Bring it to the boil. Garnish the butter chicken with the remaining chopped coriander before serving.

Tip off

If fresh cream is not available, it can be substituted by fresh *malai*.

Naan

Plain *Naan* is served straight out of the oven without butter. For Butter Naan, just spread some ghee or butter on the hot *naan*.

Naan

Ingredients

4 cups of white flour (maida)
½ tsp baking powder
1 tsp salt
½ cup milk
1 tbsp sugar
4 tbsps of oil
1 tsp of nigella seeds (kalonji)

Method

Sift the flour, salt and baking powder into a bowl and make a well in the middle. Mix the sugar, milk, and two tbsps of oil in a bowl. Pour this into the centre of the flour and knead adding water if necessary to form a soft dough. Add the remaining oil, knead again, then cover with damp cloth and allow the dough to stand for about 15 minutes. Knead the dough again and cover it, leaving it for 2-3 hours. About half an hour before the *naans* are required, turn on the oven to maximum heat. Divide the dough into eight balls and allow it to rest for 3-4 minutes. Sprinkle a baking sheet with nigella seeds and put it in the oven to heat while the dough is resting. Shape each ball of dough with the palms to make an oval shape. Bake the *naan* until puffed up and golden brown. Serve hot.

Tip off

If you are a non-vegetarian, you can add an egg in the dough along with the milk and oil. This will help in puffing up of the *naan*.

Missi Roti

Missi Roti can be cooked in an oven or tandoor or on a *tawa*.

Missi Roti

Ingredients

2 cups whole wheat flour (atta)
2 cups of gram flour (besan)
1 tsp cumin seeds
2 tbsps dry fenugreek leaves
(kasoori methi)
red chilli powder (to taste)
salt (to taste)
a pinch of turmeric powder
2 tbsps of oil
water (to knead)

Method

Put the wheat flour, gram flour, salt, chilli powder, turmeric powder in a vessel and mix well. Make a powder of the fenugreek leaves and mix it to the flour. Rub oil into the flour, and slowly add water and make a soft dough and keep it covered with damp cloth for about 30 minutes. Knead well the dough again and make the balls. Roll into a slightly thick *chapatti* than usual. Pre-heat the girdle (tawa) and cook the *missi roti* with or without oil.

Tip off

The dough of Missi Roti can also be used to make Missi Parantha.

Roomali Roti

Roomali Rotis are thin and neatly folded before serving.

Roomali Roti

Ingredients

1½ cup whole wheat flour (atta)
50 gms *maida* (white flour)
½ tsp baking powder
2 tbsps of oil
water (to knead)

Method

Mix the wheat flour, *maida* (white flour), salt and baking powder and sieve them together. Pour the oil in the flour and add water bit by bit making a smooth, elastic dough and set aside covered with moist muslin cloth for half an hour. Now make small balls of the dough and roll like a thin *chapatti* of about 12" diameter circle using little dry flour. Make sure that the *chapatti* is thin as a tissue. Heat an inverted griddle (tawa). Place the *Rumali Roti* carefully over it and cook till done. Fold it like a handkerchief.

Tip off

It requires a lot of practice before you could actually churn out the paper thin Roomali Roti. So do not lose heart. Remember practice makes a man perfect.

Lachha Parantha

The beauty of *Lachha Parantha* lies in its softness.

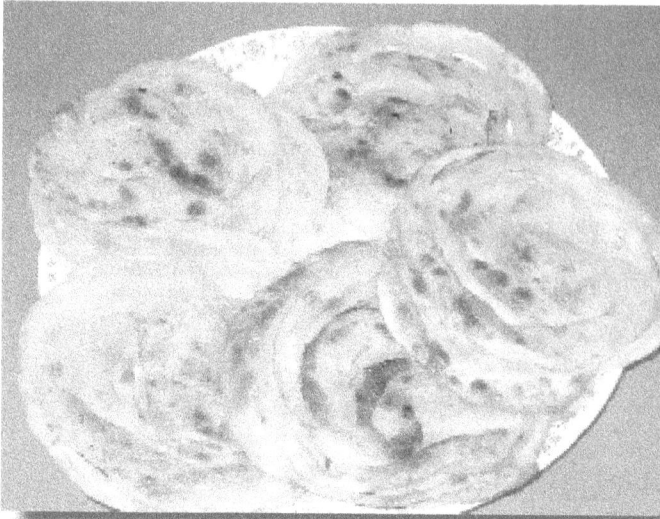

Lachha Parantha

Ingredients

whole wheat flour (atta) as per consumption
50 gms *maida* (white flour)
1 tbsp oil
salt (as per taste)
butter/ghee (pure ghee)
water (for kneading)

Method

Make a dough out of whole-wheat flour, *maida* (white flour), 1tbsp oil and salt, as you would do for any *parantha/roti*. Make a dough 30 minutes before and cover it with moist muslin cloth. Take a ping-pong ball of the size of a lump of dough. Now roll it into a circle of appoximately 5 to 6 " diameter using dry flour. Heat the ghee or oil so that it turns to liquid. Now spread the ghee properly over the entire surface. Using a knife make a 2" cut lengthways and fold it inwards. Spread the oil on every fold. Now press it lightly towards the centre to show the layers clearly and roll like a *parantha*. Cook on a pre-heated *tawa*. Turn the *lachha parantha* and pour half tablespoon oil or butter. Spread it on the *parantha* and shallow fry over low heat. Turn it and again pour oil or butter on the other side. Cook the *lachha parantha* on a low heat till golden brown.

Tip off

If you want your *lachha parantha* to be softer, add a little *malai* and two tablespoons of milk in the dough.

Vegetable Biryani

This dish of *basmati rice* combined with vegetables and dry fruits is not only appetizing but nutritious too.

Vegetable Biryani

Ingredients

2 cups of basmati rice
1 cup mixed vegetable (cauliflower, potato, carrot, French beans, etc.)
150 gms green peas
3 finely sliced onions
2 finely sliced green chillies
salt (to taste)
1 tsp red chilli powder
2 tsps cinnamon
caraway seeds
4 cloves
½ tsp black pepper powder
4 tomatoes
½ cup yogurt
4 tbsps of vegetable oil or ghee
½ tsp of mustard seeds
3 tbsps of dry fruits (cashew nuts, raisins)

Method

Wash the basmati rice well before cooking. Keep it aside for an hour. Then take rice with about two cups of water and a little salt added to it along with two tablespoons of dry fruits. Cook it in pressure cooker or in a pan or microwave. Cut all the vegetables into small thin pieces and fry each one of it separately in oil. Fry the green peas also. Take one tbsp of oil in a pan and add mustard seeds, green chillies, cinnamon and caraway seeds powder, cloves, black pepper powder and stir for about half a minute. Then add the onions and sauté them for a minute or till they get pink in colour. Add salt and red chilli powder and stir. Add the fine chopped tomatoes and fry till they are properly cooked. Take the yogurt and make it fine by putting in a blender for just two rotations. Add this fine yogurt and stir well. Heat it for about ten seconds. Add all the fried vegetables. Add the cooked rice and mix well lightly so that the rice grains do not break. Cook for about three minutes. Take this vegetable biryani out in a rice serving dish. Garnish with dry fruits and green coriander leaves.

Tip off

Serve the vegetable biryani hot with raita made up of curd and pickle.

Mughlai Biryani

This biryani will bring back the Mughal era in your dining room.

Mughlai Biryani

Ingredients

500 gms basmati rice
50 pieces almonds
500 gms meat (chicken or mutton)
4 red chillies
125 gms onion
10 mint leaves
200 gms curd
5 green chillies
100 ml milk
4 potatoes
1 lime
2 big tomatoes
Ghee or refined oil, cumin seeds, salt, ginger, garlic, coriander leaves and pinch of saffron (as per taste)

Method

Clean and wash the meat. Chop the onions. Chop the coriander and mint leaves. Grind the garlic, ginger, red and green chillies to a paste. Keep the meat for one and a half hours mixed in curd and spices. Put the ghee or oil in a cooker and fry the onions well. Take it out and put the spices and meat in a cooker. Fry. Add the salt and a cup of water. Close the cooker and cook for about ten minutes after the pressure reaches the optimum level. Let the steam out and open the cooker fast. Take out the spiced meat. Put the rice and the three and a half cups of water in the cooker. Close the cooker and cook for two minutes after the pressure reaches the optimum level. After two minutes, let the steam out and open the cooker fast. Take out the rice and put ghee in the cooker. Add ground cloves, cardamom, aniseeds, coriander, mint, almonds and salt. Carefully mix the rice with these spices, squeeze the lime juice and mix well. Dissolve the saffron in milk and add to half of the rice.

Tip off

Mughlai Biryani may be served with raita and onion rings.

Egg Tomato Rice

This plate of *pulao* decorated with eggs and tomatoes will be a special dish for your guests.

Egg Tomato Rice

Ingredients

1½ cup basmati rice
6 eggs
1 tsp sugar
½ cup crushed cottage cheese (paneer)
½ cup tomato sauce
2 big onions
1 big potato
coriander leaves
green chillies
salt and ghee (as per taste)

Method

Put the ghee in a vessel and fry the chopped onions. Add the washed rice. Put salt and enough water for the rice to boil partially and the water evaporates. Divide the rice into two parts and put in two separators of the cooker. Cut the tomatoes into halves and empty the centre. Make three hollows in rice. Make space in the separator with hand and place the bowl like tomatoes in them. Now break an egg and place it without beating, in a tomato bowl. The yellow of the egg should be inside the bowl. The white may spread around it. Now sprinkle the grated cottage cheese (paneer), chopped green chillies, chopped coriander leaves and salt mixed together. Then taking the middle of three eggs as centre, draw deep dividing lines on the rice and fill the lines with tomato sauce. Repeat the same in the other separator.

Put a little water in the cooker and place a grind. Fix both the separators on it and close the cooker. Remove from fire as soon as the pressure reaches the required level and cook the rice in the steam till the heat subsides. Take out round chunks of set rice carefully and place them straight on two plates. Decorate with fried potato rings. Put a ring of chopped coriander leaves around the rice on the plates.

Tip off

In this dish, lines filled with tomato sauce and the quantity of eggs may be altered for various kinds of decorations.

Spanish Rice

This Spanish rice is very tasty to eat and attractive to look at.

Spanish Rice

Ingredients

2 cups basmati rice
1 cup boiled spaghetti or macaroni
2 tbsps of sugar
¼ cup tomato sauce
200 gms capsicums
2 medium sized onions
cottage cheese (paneer)
garlic
ginger
garam masala
salt and ghee (as per taste)

Method

Put ghee or butter in a cooker and fry the sugar till brown in colour. This will give a colouring to the rice. Now fry thin slices of onions, garlic and ginger. Wash the rice and add to it. Fry for some time. Add salt and water. It will be a brown coloured *pulao* when cooked.

Fry pieces of capsicum in ghee separately. Put a pinch of salt and tomato sauce. Take out the rice from the cooker (it should not be fully cooked at this stage). Put one layer of rice, then a layer of capsicum mixed with tomato sauce on top of it. Repeat this three or four times. Close the cooker and steam the rice till fully done.

Garnishing: Put rice on the sides of a big platter with a hollow in the middle. Fill it with boiled *spaghetti* or *macaroni*. Decorate with lines of tomato sauce, cottage cheese and finely chopped coriander leaves garnishing for different designs.

Tip off

You may cook these rice dishes in a rice cooker for better results.

Dahi Vada

Dahi Vada is a special curd preparation which is equally liked by children and adults.

Dahi Vada

Ingredients

For Vada:
1 cup *urad dal* (black gram)
salt (to taste)
oil (to fry)

For Dahi :
1 kg *dahi* (yogurt or curd)
½ tsp grated ginger
finely chopped coriander leaves
1-2 green chillies chopped
salt (to taste)
2 tsps roasted cumin (jeera)
powder
red chilli powder (to taste)

Method

Clean, wash and soak the *urad dal* (black gram) overnight. Grind it into smooth paste. Add salt to taste. Heat the oil in a pan and drop spoonfuls of batter and fry till golden brown. Take the hot *vadas* and put in cold water for 20 - 30 minutes. Now take them out of water and squeeze the water, keeping aside. Blend the curd (yogurt) and little water until it is smooth. Keep them in the refrigerator for an hour to get chilled. Add salt, red chilli powder and cumin powder. In a deep dish, arrange the *vada* and pour the *dahi* (curd) over them. Now add the green mint *chutney*. Garnish with coriander. Serve the *dahi vadas* chilled.

Tip off

If you like your *dahi vadas* to be sweet, then you may pour sweet tamarind *chutney* (saunth) over the the *dahi vada* before serving.

Bathue ka Raita

Bathue ka Raita is eaten in winters as *bathua* provides warmth to the body.

Ingredients

1 cup curd (yogurt)
½ cup *bathua* (boiled and mashed)
1tsp roasted cumin (jeera) powder
salt (to taste)
red chilli powder (to taste)

Bathue ka Raita

Method

Stir the curd with hand mixer (mathani) or with a spoon vigorously. Add the *bathua* paste made in a mixie or grinded manually and mix well. If it becomes thick, add little milk and mix it. Now add salt, cumin powder and chilli powder. Then mix it well again. Keep in the refrigerator for an hour or so. Serve the chilled *bathue ka raita* with rice, *paranthas*, etc.

Tip off

Use some boiled and mashed *bathua* as *parantha* filling and relish it with *bathue ka raita*.

Fruit Raita

Fruit Raita is healthy and a boon to those who like to keep a count of their calories.

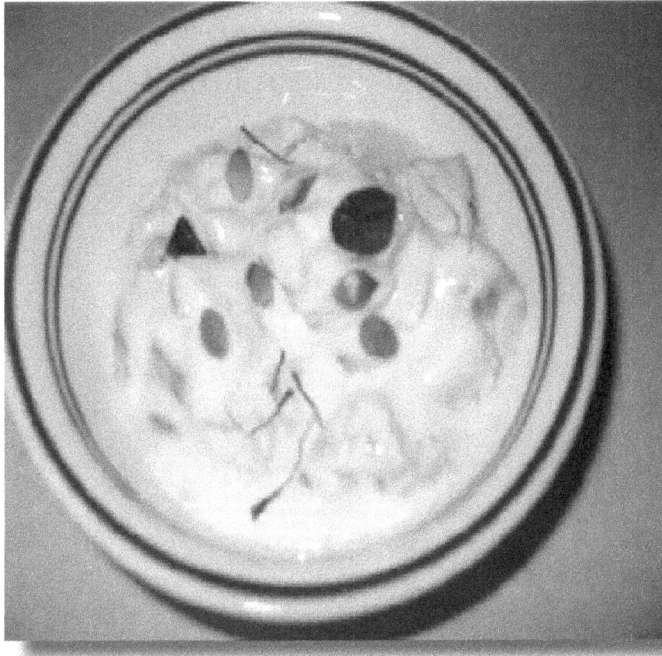

Ingredients

2 cups curd (yogurt)
3 bananas
1 small pineapple
2 apples
1 or 2 ripe mangoes
1 cup pomegranate seeds
chopped coriander leaves
sugar (to taste)
salt (to taste)
black pepper powder (to taste)
papaya pieces (optional)

Fruit Raita

Method

Stir the curd with hand mixer (Mathni) or in a mixie properly and mix salt and sugar in the curd. If the curd is thick, add little milk or water. Cut all the fruits in small cubes and add to the curd. Garnish the fruit raita with chopped coriander and pomegranate.

Tip off

You may add any number of your choice of fruits to the raita to make it more delicious.

Salad Dressing

This dressing makes plain and simple salad delicious.

Ingredients

3 tsps cornflour
1 cup milk
1 tsp sugar
salt (to taste)
1 tbsp vinegar
¼ tsp mustard

Salad Dressing

Method

Dissolve three small spoons of corn flour in a little water. Heat a cup of milk and add to it. Cook for about three minutes stirring all the time. Let it cool. Now add a teaspoon of sugar, salt and a little mustard to a tablespoon of vinegar and add this mixture to the salad or serve separately. This will add the flavour, taste and look of your salad. Try it out!

Tip off

Salads are generally nutritious and low on calories.

French Dressing

As the name suggests, this dressing imparts a special flavour to the dish, as well as adds to the taste too!

Ingredients

1 tsp lemon juice
3 tsps of salad oil
2 tsps of ground onion
1 tsp ground garlic
1 tsp ground mustard
1 tsp red chilli powder
salt and black pepper (to taste)

French Dressing

Method

Mix a spoon of lemon juice to three spoons of salad oil. Now add two spoons of ground onions, one spoon of ground garlic, one spoon of ground mustard, one spoon of red chilli powder or half a spoon of black pepper and salt to it, according to your taste. Leave it for one hour. Then take out and use.

Your French Dressing of your salad can be prepared – making your salad, all the more attractive and delicious.

Tip off

Instead of lemon juice, three spoons of vinegar can also be added.

Salad Boats

This boat shaped salads will get you a lot of appreciation. Place them in the centre of the dining table before serving the food.

Salad Boats

Ingredients

1 middle-sized gourd
2 potatoes
2 cloves
some toothpicks
1 tomato
1 radish
1 cucumber
1 beetroot

Method

Take a middle sized long gourd. Slit it in halves and take out the pulp from one half. It will be in the shape of a boat. Use this as a plate to decorate the salad on it.

Boil a big long and another almond sized potato. Before they become too tender, take out and peel. Cut the bottom of the big potato, so that it can stand on its own. Fix the small potato on the big potato with a toothpick in such a way that it looks like the head and body of the doll. Put two cloves to make the eyes. Cut the flowered side of a clove and use it for the nose and place the fine slices of tomato skin to make the lips. Dress the doll up with a shirt and scarf made of lettuce. For hands, cut two long strips of radish and shove them in the potato making the body. A belle from Kashmir is ready to ply her boat. Place two sticks in the doll's hands like two oars. You can make anything else with your imagination.

Now whatever ingredients you have for salad – cucumbur, radish, tender radish leaves, carrot, beetroot, tomato, etc., cut them in shapes of flowers and leaves. Fill up the boat with them.

Tip off

Your guests will be delighted to see a boat full of flowers and fruits, sailing on a lake and the Kashmiri belle selling flowers and fruits.

Radish Swans Salad

The decoration of this salad makes it different and unique from others and is highly appetizing.

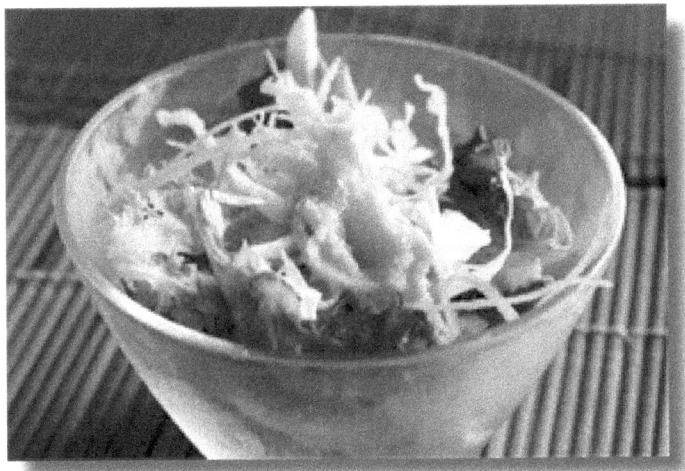

Radish Swans Salad

Ingredients

2 radish
2 tomatoes
1 cucumber
2 carrots
1 onion
4-5 cloves

Method

Select the radish which has edges that resemble the mouth of a swan, or cut the edges a little to give it a shape. Insert two cloves to make the eyes. Make wings out of lettuce. Bore with a pin and fix the wings with toothpicks. Place two radish swans on two sides of a big plate and decorate the middle with tomato, cucumber, carrot, etc. Keep the tomatoes whole. Slit them from four sides to look like a big blooming flower. Carrot, cucumber, onion, etc. can be cut into the shapes of small flowers and leaves or in rings. Serve mint *chutney* or salad dressing separately. You can also serve this salad with white sauce.

Tip off

Let your imagination run wild and prepare different types of salads in different shapes, giving them different tastes.

A Bouquet of Salad

You must have seen many flower bouquets, but here's a bouquet of salad. Interesting and alluring, isn't it?

Ingredients

some lettuce leaves
1 cabbage
1 carrot
2 boiled potatoes
1 beetroot
2 tomatoes
100 gms cottage
cheese (paneer)
1 radish
some mint and coriander leaves
1 lemon
green chillies
black pepper (to taste)

A Bouquet of Salad

Method

Take a deep plate or a container similar to a basket. First place the lettuce or a cabbage leaf on all the sides. In the middle, put the chopped tender leaves from the middle portion of a cabbage, small pieces of carrot, boiled potatoes, beetroot, tomato slices, pieces of cottage cheese (paneer), radish, chopped mint and coriander leaves and fill them up till the top. Put the dressing on top, squeeze a lemon into juice and sprinkle black pepper, salt and chopped green chillies.

Tip off

This salad bouquet will look lovely and mouth-watering in the centre of the table.

Salad Decoration

Salad decorations should not be for your guests only, but should be a part of your daily menu.

Salad Decoration

Ingredients

some lettuce leave
some radish leaves
2-3 carrots
2-3 radish
½ cup boiled peas
1 cucumber
2 onions
chopped coriander leaves
1 tsp lemon juice
salt and black pepper (to taste)

Method

Take a leaf shaped, dark coloured plate. To begin with, place two long strips of radish on the uneven side of the plate like two broad leaves. Lettuce cut in similar shape can also be used. Decorate a tomato, cut in the shape of a flower along with lettuce or radish leaves on the pointed side of the plate. Cut a radish leaf in the shape of a small mango and place it in the middle of the plate. Now arrange two rows of shelled boiled peas around it. Decorate the radish, carrot, cucumber (whatever you want to use) after cutting in the shape of flowers all around and place the plate on a stand. Garnish the middle portion of the salad with chopped coriander and squeeze the juice of half of a lemon on top. Salt and black pepper can be sprinkled if desired according to your taste. A lovely plate of salad is ready.

The above are only suggestions. You can evolve many artistic ways of decorating salads, using your imagination. Do experiment and serve the same vegetables used in salads, but in different and attractive ways, so that those who do not have a special liking for vegetables will be allured towards them and cultivate the habit of eating salads.

Tip off

Salads are a must for the health and nutrition of your family.

Sweet Dilbahar

Sweet Dilbahar is a light and tasty dessert.

Ingredients

250 gms cottage cheese (paneer)
200 gms thickened milk
300 gms sugar
1 tsp semolina
chopped dry fruits
cardamoms
1 or 2 tbsps of ghee or butter

Sweet Dilbahar

Method

Curdle a litre of buffalo or cow's milk with lemon juice and prepare cottage cheese or *paneer* at home. It will be about 250 gms, in quantity. Place it under a heavy stone to set. Then crush it and add one spoon of semolina. Take 100 gms of sugar. Now make cakes out of the cottage cheese, immerse in a syrup prepared with sugar, drops of milk and water and let it cook till the syrup is thick enough for setting. Take out the *paneer* cakes and spread them separately. They will dry up when cool. Cut them into two parts from the middle.

Heat one or two big spoons of ghee or butter in a vessel and fry the thickened milk on low fire. Add chopped dry fruits, cardamoms and take off from the fire. Mix 100 gms of ground sugar.

Now pick up the two parts of cottage cheese cakes. Place the thickened milk mixture in the middle and press one part against another. A tasty and attractive looking new kind of sweet is ready for your guests. Enjoy eating it.

Tip off

This heart shaped sweet tastes good
with or without the milk filling.

Tricolour Cakes

This special dessert has a unique taste and appearance.

Tricolour Cakes

Ingredients

8 slices of bread
1 cup milk
200 gms of cottage cheese
(paneer)
250 gms sugar
a few pieces of *cherry murabba*
or simple cherries
ghee or butter (for frying)

Method

Scrape the red edges of the bread slices and cut them in rounds from the centre. Pour milk on a big shallow plate. Heat ghee or butter in a vessel or a non-stick frying pan. Soak each piece of bread in milk from all sides and take out before it gets soggy and fry them on high flame in heated ghee. Soak the fried pieces in syrup and take out immediately. Add two spoons of milk to the remaining syrup. Strain after the dirt separates. Now make round cakes of cottage cheese (should be half the size of bread cakes) and cook them in the syrup. When the syrup starts setting, take off from the fire and place the cakes on the fried bread cakes immediately. They will set when cool. Place a cherry on top of each cottage cheese cake while still hot. All the three parts will stick to each other after the cake is cool. Decorate them on a plate and serve.

Tip off

Cherry murabba can be substituted with pieces of canned pineapple and cherries.

Cottage Cheese Murgi

This sweet made of only cottage cheese (paneer) is great to eat and nutritious as well as energy-giving.

Cottage Cheese Murgi

Ingredients

About 2 litres of milk
500 gms sugar or more, if required
1 tsp cardamom seeds (ground)

Method

Curdle about two litres of pure buffalo milk or cow's milk with the juice of two lemons. Strain in a cloth and drain water. Make it into one lump and keep it under a flat, heavy stone. After it sets like a plate, cut into small pieces and spread on a cloth, till the water evaporates completely. Now make one string of sugar syrup. Add all the pieces and ground the cardamoms. Keep on stirring till each cardamom piece dries up and separates. Decorate it on a dark coloured pretty plate or bowl and serve.

Tip off

Instead of making cottage cheese (paneer) at home, you can buy it from the market. In that case — buy around 350-400 gms of paneer.

Coconut Burfi

Coconut imparts a special flavour and taste to various dishes. Here's a dessert, especially for coconut lovers.

Coconut Burfi

Ingredients

1 middle-sized raw coconut
½ kg thickened milk
1 kg sugar
1 tbsp ghee or butter

Method

Peel the coconut and grate. Fry the thickened milk in a little ghee or butter in a separate utensil. It should not turn red. Make the sugar syrup in another vessel. When it is of one string consistency, add the grated coconut and cook. When the syrup thickens to 3 strings consistency and ready to set, add the thickened milk and keep on stirring. Grease a plate with ghee or butter and transfer this mixture on it to set. The *Burfi* will be set after it cools. Cut pieces with a knife. These should also be decorated on a dark coloured plate with rose petals, if you like. If raw coconut is not available, dry grated coconut can be used instead. It will not be necessary to cook it in the syrup. Add the thick syrup with the thickened milk directly and leave it to set. This will add to the taste of the *Burfi*.

Tip off

This burfi can be eaten during fasts as well, as it doesnot contain salt, cereals or pulses.

Ras Bada

Ras Bada is different from other sweets like *gulab jamun* or *rasogulla* in hardness and consistency.

Ras Bada

Ingredients

250 gms ground *urad dal* (black grams)
1 cup mild
500 gms thickened milk
500 gms sugar
chopped dry fruits
ghee or butter (for frying)

Method

Grind the *urad dal* or black grams and make into flour or soak it overnight and grind to a paste in the morning. Add dry fruits, thickened milk and make into big round cakes. Make a hole in the middle of each cake and fry in heated oil or ghee in a vessel. Flame should be low to fry the cakes properly. Now make one string sugar syrup and dip the hot cakes in it. Fill up the holes with cashew nuts and decorate on a plate. More cashew nuts can be put on the plate, if desired.

Tip off

You can also add almonds, raisins and pistachio along with cashew nuts for garnishing.

Moong Burfi

This *burfi* may be yellow or green in colour depending upon the *dal* or pulse used which may be washed *moong* or *whole moong dal* (green grams) respectively.

Ingredients

250 gms whole moong or green grams
250 gms thickened milk
250 gms ghee or butter
500 gms ground sugar
chopped dry fruits
cardamom seeds

Moong Burfi

Method

Clean the *moong dal* and grind in to a coarse flour.

Put the ghee or butter in a vessel and fry this flour on low heat. When the ghee or butter separates, add the thickened milk and fry for about five minutes. Take off from the fire and add the chopped dry fruits, cardamoms, ground sugar and set on a plate or any vessel of your choice. After it sets, cut pieces out of it and decorate on a plate.

Tip off

Green burfis can be made with pistachio in a similar way. But because of the high price of pistachios, you may only decorate the yellow Moong Burfi with a few cashew nuts and raisins, as per your choice.

Royal Toasts

This dessert is simple and easy to make. It is very tasty too!

Royal Toasts

Ingredients

8 slices of bread
6 tsps of sugar
½ a litre milk
1 piece of coconut
8 pieces of *cherry murabba*
1 pinch yellow colouring
ghee or butter (for frying)

Method

Cut about seven or eight slices of bread in diamond shape using a sharp knife. Fry them in ghee or butter in a vessel or a frying pan. Now, remove before they turn pink. Cut the ninth piece in a round shape using the lid of a bottle. Fry this also.

Thicken milk by boiling it for some time in a vessel. Add sugar, grated coconut and take it off the fire. Decorate the seven or eight big slices on a plate in the shape of a star. Place the round piece in the centre and make the shape even. Now spread the thickened milk on the seven or eight slices, leaving two centimetre space between them. Take two small spoons of sugar, 2 spoons of water and yellow sweet colouring with the help of a thin stick. Decorate a cherry in the centre of each toast.

Tip off

You may further beautify this plate by filling up the empty spaces in the plate with uneven leaves, cut out of green paper. Guests will be pleased to see this dish as well as find it delicious to eat.

Carrot Halwa

Carrots are available in plenty during winter. It is a cheap vegetable, richest in food values. Its nutritional value goes up if mixed with milk and this tasty dish for breakfast is liked by everybody.

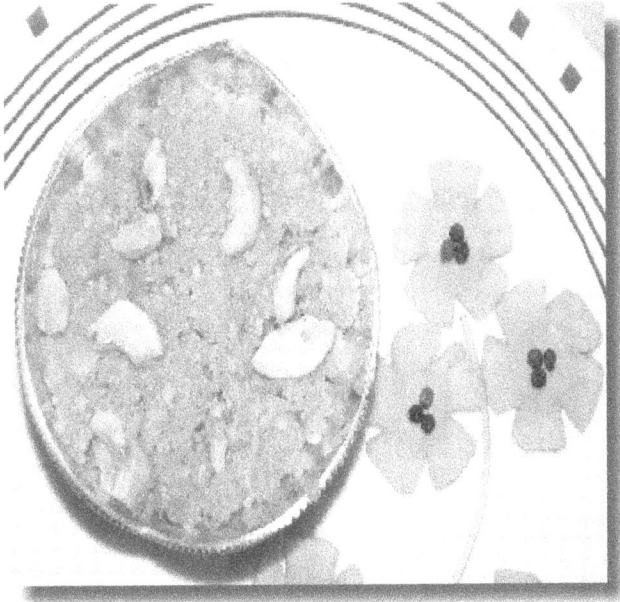

Carrot Halwa

Ingredients

1 kg carrots
1 litre of milk
2 or 3 tbsps ghee/butter
sugar (as per taste)
1 cup raisins, cashew nuts and almonds

Method

Scrape the outside of one kilo carrots. Clean and wash them well. Then grate them. Put on the fire with about one litre milk. Let it boil for four or five times on high flame. Add sugar in the end and cook on low fire. Ghee or butter can be added as per taste. After the water and milk evaporate, cook on low fire for a little while. Transfer on a plate and decorate with cashew nuts, raisins and almonds or with raisins and cashew nuts only. Floral or leafy designs for decoration will make the dish look more attractive. Keep a money plant near the tray to give the table a lovely look.

Tip off

Carrot is rich in vitamin A. It is particularly very beneficial for the eyes.

Semolina Halwa

This nutritious, sweet preparation for breakfast can be made very fast.

Semolina Halwa

Ingredients

1 cup semolina (suji)
2 tbsps of ghee or butter
2 cups of sugar
some cardamom seeds and raisins or
cashew nuts, almonds, etc.
for garnishing

Method

Put the sugar in water and heat. After one boil, strain the syrup and keep aside. Put just enough ghee or butter in a vessel to soak the semolina. Fry the semolina on low fire till pink in colour. When the ghee separates, lower the flame further and add the syrup. Then put the flame up and stir the *halwa* fast. Add the cardamom seeds and raisins during cooking, so that the raisins become fluffy and the *halwa* has a cardamom flavour. Saffron may be added to make the *kesaris* out of this *halwa*. Transfer the *halwa* on plates and garnish with chopped dry fruits of your choice. Decorate it with silver wrapper, chopped dry fruits and cashew powder. This will certainly make the sweet dish look more attractive.

Tip off

Moong dal flour can be used instead of semolina to prepare *halwa* in the same way. But *halwa* made with fresh fried batter of soaked *dal* is tastier. The *dal* batter should be fried on low fire for a long time, sprinkling ghee occasionally.

Ice Cream

Ice cream can be prepared in many ways. Here are given three good formulae:

Ice Cream

Ingredients

½ litre of milk
custard powder
½ kg sugar
2-3 eggs
100 gms fresh cream
mango, coffee, chocolate powder
a pinch of salt
1 tsp of gelatine

Method

Formula 1: Make custard with half of litre milk and a packet of custard powder. Let it cool. Mash the pulp of one big mango, or extract juice of four small mangoes and mix. Dissolve about one spoon of gelatine in two spoons of hot water. Cool and mix with it. Add the sugar as per taste and whip and refrigerate to set. Take out after an hour. Whip about 100 gms of cream and mix with it. Whip again the entire mixture and refrigerate to set.

Formula 2: Make a cup of coffee, or dissolve the chocolate powder and let it cool. Keep a cup of cream ready beforehand. Beat the yolk of three eggs lightly. Add a cup of sugar, a pinch of salt, half of the cream and coffee or chocolate with it and beat. Cook this mixture on steam. Add the remaining cream after it is cool and beat again. Now refrigerate to set.

Formula 3: Whip the yolk of two eggs with half a litre of milk to make custard. Add sugar and let it cool. Whip 100 gms of cream and add. Beat the entire mixture again. Dissolve one spoon of gelatine in about two cups of hot water and add to the mixture after it is cool. Refrigerate. Take it out after an hour when three-fourth is set. Beat the remaining white of the eggs and add to it. Now beat the whole ice cream again and leave it to set. Delicious ice cream, will be ready after one and a half hour to two hours. Serve the ice cream in cups, decorated with crepe waters.

Tip off

Pour some chocolate syrup on top of the cooled ice cream to add to its beauty, flavour ad taste.

Kulfi

Cool *kulfi* tastes amazing and very refreshing in the summer heat.

Ingredients

1 litre milk
½ cup sugar
½ cup chopped dry fruits
2 tsps of rose water (optional)
½ lemon

Kulfi

Method

Boil about one litre of milk and leave it on low flame to thicken till half the quantity, or you may mix one cup of milk with one cup of whipped cream. Add about half a cup of sugar, chopped dry fruits, two spoons rose water or a few drops of essence. Add the juice of half a small lemon or one-fourth of a big one. Put the mixture in moulds, seal them with dough of refined flour or wheat flour and refrigerate. (Lemon juice will prevent crystal formation). After some time, delicious *kulfi* will be ready for use. If refrigeration facility is not available, fill up a mud pitcher with pieces of ice. Add a pinch of salt to it and bury the *kulfi* moulds in ice. Shake the pitcher occasionally. The *kulfi* will get set after a while.

Tip off

You may add condensed milk available in the market to make the kulfi rich in essence, sweeter and tastier.

Fruit Custard

This is a popular sweet dish served after a meal.

Ingredients

1 litre of milk
1 cup custard powder
1 cup mixed cut fruits
1 tsp rose water (optional)
sugar (to taste)

Fruit Custard

Method

Dissolve one cup of custard powder in half a cup of water. Boil half a litre of milk and add the custard to it, stirring all the time. Add the sugar when thick and take off from the fire. Spread a layer of grapes and other fruit pieces (apple, chikoo, banana, papaya, etc.,) in a bowl and cover with a layer of custard. Repeat this several times. Fill up the bowl with three or four such layers and keep in the fridge. A little rose water may also be added, if one likes. The custard will set even without refrigeration, though it takes a little longer.

Tip off

If after refrigeration, the custard becomes too thick, then add one or two teaspoons of cold milk to it and mix it properly.

Fruit Cream

After a delicious meal (lunch or dinner), a fruit cream is like an icing on a cake.

Fruit Cream

Ingredients

1 cup whipped cream
1cup mixed cut fruits
1 tsp rose water
1 tsp peeled almonds
5-6 cherries

Method

Any available sweet fruits like, papaya, mango, leechee, grapes, etc., can be used. Wash, deseed and cut them in small pieces. Add one cup of whipped cream in a bowl of cut fruits. Sprinkle a little rose water (optional). Add grapes and a few pieces of peeled almonds and raisins. Decorate with cherries on top.

Tip off

Serve the fruit cream in special glass bowls to look more tantalizing.

Patato Chocolate Pudding

This combination of potatoes and chocolate in a dessert is unique.

Potato Chocolate Pudding

Ingredients

125 gms potatoes
2 eggs
25 gms cooking chocolate
60 gms butter
3 tsps cornflour
¼ tsp baking powder
2 cardamoms
chopped almonds, raisins and
cherries (as per taste)

Method

Boil the potatoes and mash. Whip the chocolate and cornflour in a little water and add milk. Whip the eggs and add slowly, whipping all the time. Add sugar. Now mix the butter and mashed potatoes also. Add the chopped almonds and ground cardamom seeds. Put the mixture in an airtight vessel and cook on steam. Put two cups of water in the cooker. Put a grid and place the pudding vessel on top. Close the cooker and cook for about 20 minutes after the pressure attains the required limit. Decorate with cherries, chopped almonds and raisins before serving.

Tip off

This pudding can be baked in an oven also. This will definitely give a unique and different taste.

CAREER & BUSINESS MANAGEMENT

Also Available
in Hindi, Kannada

Also Available
in Hindi, Kannada

Also Available in Kannada

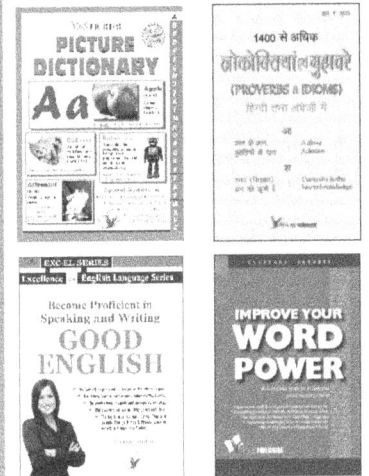

STUDENT DEVELOPMENT/LEARNING

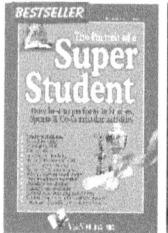

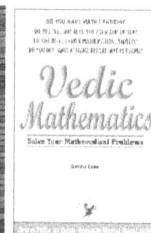

POPULAR SCIENCE

GREATEST CRAFTS PROJECTS for CHILDREN

WONDERS of the World

RAMAYANA

BESTSELLER
7 अच्छे अंकों से परीक्षा पास करने के 7 रहस्य

7 Mantras to Excel in EXAMS

71 Electrical & Electronic Projects

Children's SCIENCE ENCYCLOPEDIA

Also Available in Hindi

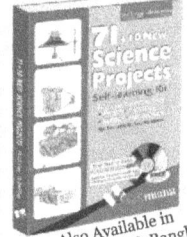

BESTSELLER
Super Student

आप भी मेरिट में आ सकते हैं

251 STUDY SECRETS

Vedic Mathematics
Solve Your Mathematical Problems

वैदिक गणित

Science

NEW
71 + 10 New Mathematics Projects

Also Available in Hindi

Also Available in Hindi

Learning MATHEMATICS the Fun Way

वाद-विवाद (DEBATE)

निबन्ध संग्रह

Enhance Your Child's Talents

Stories for Children

71 Science Projects Junior

71 Science Experiments

Also Available in Hindi

Also Available in Hindi

PUZZLES

MATHEMAGIC Puzzles & Brain Drainers

SUDOKU

SUDOKU

SUDOKU

Mind Benders Brain Teasers
150

101 + 10 New SCIENCE GAMES

71 + 10 New Science Projects

Also Available in Hindi

Also Available in Hindi, Tamil & Bangla

DRAWING BOOKS

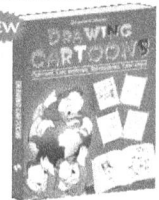

ड्राइंग एण्ड पेंटिंग कोर्स

Drawing & Painting Course

Drawing & Painting Course Volume II

ड्राइंग कार्टून्स

NEW
DRAWING CARTOONS

Space Science
The best of Science Funnies

71 ARTS & CRAFTS FOR SCHOOL CHILDREN

71 + 10 Magic Tricks for Children

CHILDREN'S ENCYCLOPEDIA – THE WORLD OF KNOWLEDGE

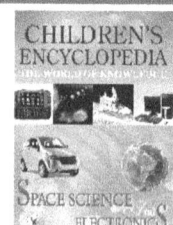

CHILDREN'S ENCYCLOPEDIA THE WORLD OF KNOWLEDGE

CHILDREN'S ENCYCLOPEDIA THE WORLD OF KNOWLEDGE
GENERAL KNOWLEDGE

CHILDREN'S ENCYCLOPEDIA THE WORLD OF KNOWLEDGE
LIFE SCIENCES and HUMAN BODY

CHILDREN'S ENCYCLOPEDIA THE WORLD OF KNOWLEDGE
PHYSICS and CHEMISTRY

CHILDREN'S ENCYCLOPEDIA THE WORLD OF KNOWLEDGE
SCIENTIFIC PRINCIPLES and DISCOVERIES

CHILDREN'S ENCYCLOPEDIA THE WORLD OF KNOWLEDGE
SPACE SCIENCE and ELECTRONICS

Contact us at sales@vspublishers.com

HINDI LITERATURE

MUSIC/MYSTERIES/MAGIC & FACT

Also Available in Hindi

TALES & STORIES

All Books Fully Coloured

OTHER BOOKS

Also available in Hindi

CHILDREN TALES (बच्चों की कहानियाँ)

BANGLA LANGUAGE (बांग्ला भाषा)

   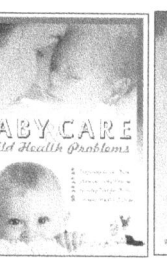   

GENERAL HEALTH & BEAUTY CARE

FITNESS

PERFECT HEALTH & AYURVEDA

A Set of 4 Books

DISEASES & COMMON AILMENTS

REGIONAL LANGUAGE

(Telugu)　　(Odia)　　(Marathi)　　(Bangla)

All books available at www.vspublishers.com

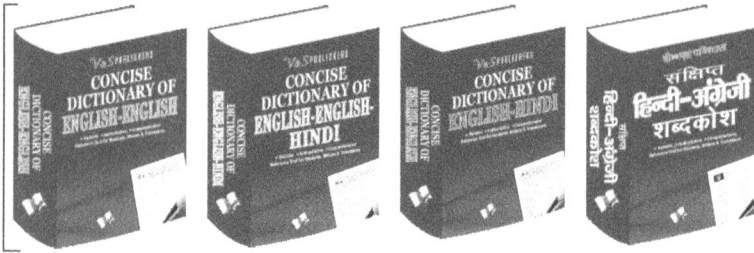

www.ingramcontent.com/pod-product-compliance
Lightning Source LLC
Chambersburg PA
CBHW081420270326
41931CB00015B/3353